"Everyone should have
their mind blown once a day."
—Neil deGrasse Tyson

# STARSTRUCK

## The Cosmic Journey of Neil deGrasse Tyson

### Kathleen Krull and Paul Brewer

#### Illustrated by Frank Morrison

Crown Books for Young Readers
New York

OUR UNIVERSE BEGAN its dance with what scientists call the Big Bang. After many millions of years of darkness, spots of impossible brightness—stars—sizzled into shape. Some grew so massive that they exploded, spewing star dust every which way. **BOOM.**

The star dust contained what was needed to create more shapes, more patterns, the planets, our whole universe.

Zoom forward almost 13.8 billion years to the sky theater at the Hayden Planetarium, in New York City. On the domed ceiling, the planets and constellations created by the Big Bang pulsed against the black ink of space.

Nine-year-old Neil deGrasse Tyson had never seen so many stars. After all, from his apartment in the Bronx, it looked like there were only about twelve. Now above him were what seemed like millions—too many to possibly be real. Was this a hoax, a joke?

He wasn't sure, but when the lights came on, his thoughts began to explode. "The universe called me," he said simply. And he would never be the same.

Starstruck, Neil started looking up whenever he could. Even though he lived in an apartment building named Skyview, his view of the night sky wasn't very good. Too many bright city lights got in the way.

His good friend Phillip lent him a pair of binoculars. Neil used them to peer at the moonscape over the Hudson River, the glossy orb with its craters and shadows. "And it came alive," he marveled.

On a family trip out of the city, away from all the lights, he was able to see more. Sure enough, the night sky really did look like the one at the Hayden Planetarium. It was real! The sheer wonder of it all, the blinding beauty, the mysteries just waiting to be solved, fascinated him.

Neil was hooked. He had a whole new goal. Becoming a baseball player was out. Now he was going to be . . . an astrophysicist, a scientist who studies the universe!

Neil's parents weren't scientists and they weren't rich, but they did everything they could to help. For his twelfth birthday, they bought him a telescope.

Atop the twenty stories of Skyview, he examined the night sky in all its glimmering glory.

His parents also bought him every science book on sale so he could learn about what he was looking at. Neil had one of the biggest libraries of any kid at school.

His knowledge of the stars began to explode.

The more Neil learned, the more he thirsted to know. But he needed a bigger, better telescope—one that cost more money than his parents could afford.

Neil solved his own problem. He offered to walk his neighbors' dogs for pay. These were pampered city dogs with cute names like Tuffy. On rainy days, some of them even wore their own raincoats and boots.

Eventually, he saved enough money to buy a five-foot-long telescope with his parents' help.

Neil headed back up to the roof. Sometimes people saw him up there and were afraid. What was an African American boy doing on the roof? Was his long telescope really a rifle? Was he an armed robber? Often, they called the police.

Neil solved this problem, too. When police officers stopped by, he would offer them the view from his telescope. He showed off the stars—like powdered sugar flung against black velvet. He would point out his favorite planet, Saturn.

Saturn just blew his mind. With its dozens of moons and its stunning, elaborate rings, it was the most gorgeous thing he'd ever seen.

The police officers would usually end up won over.

It turned out Neil could make others starstruck, too.

Neil loved school—he loved to learn. But not every teacher was his fan. "Your son laughs too loud," one told his mom. On his report cards, they complained that he spent more time talking to friends than paying attention.

But his sixth-grade teacher noticed something. Every single book report he wrote had to do with astronomy. She told him about a class at the Hayden Planetarium: Advanced Topics in Astronomy for Young People.

Neil took the subway to classes at the planetarium by himself. He was often the youngest person, and some information sailed right over his head. But he wouldn't quit, pushing himself to learn more and more.

HAYDEN PLANETARIUM

Neil's quest to understand the cosmos made him a young star at the planetarium. The director of education was so impressed that he invited Neil on an unbelievable journey to the coast of northwest Africa. An ocean liner was being turned into a floating laboratory to view a total solar eclipse. Two thousand scientists and observers, including famous astronauts and science-fiction writers, were making the two-week trip.

At fourteen, his trusty telescope in hand, Neil was the youngest scientist on board. Observing and studying the eclipse alongside expert scientists made him feel like a science superhero. Then, on the way home, he won the dance contest, and the trivia contest (thanks to his knowledge of Saturn)—the perfect ending to his first expedition.

After passing tough tests, he made it into the Bronx High School of Science. He was "a card-carrying nerd kid"—winning the science fair prizes and subscribing to the brainy *Scientific American* magazine. In the lab, he was trying not to blow things up. In his physics classes, he was getting to know the universe.

His life wasn't *all* science. He excelled at dance—from ballet to ballroom—and was captain of the wrestling team. He even used his understanding of physics to win his matches.

When he was fifteen, Neil got to go to a summer astronomy camp in the Mojave Desert in Southern California.

Scorpions, tarantulas, and howling coyotes? No problem. This was bliss. Days were full of classes on the subjects he loved. Nights were for observing with high-powered telescopes.

So far from city lights, the stars burst with more radiance and in much greater number than he'd seen since that first visit to the Hayden Planetarium. It was too inspiring for words. But with his dog-walking money, he'd also bought a good camera for taking sky pictures.

He used the camera to bring home the galaxies, constellations, moons, and planets he captured on film and shared his pictures with fifty adults at his first public talk at City College of New York.

Was he nervous? No—talking about science was "like breathing." And people liked his explosive excitement. A career in astrophysics was Neil's only goal. Many people noticed his ability and pushed him forward.

Some didn't. He often had to cope with racism. Neil even had friends who thought a future as an athlete or a leader in the African American community would be better goals for Neil than becoming a scientist.

But Neil had a strength burning inside, a flaming passion. He pictured it as a tank of rocket fuel, and every new discovery—like seeing Saturn through a telescope for the first time—poured fuel into that tank.

By the time he was starting to pick a college, his reputation in the scientific community was growing. The most famous scientist of his day, the astronomer Carl Sagan, hoped to convince Neil to come to his school.

One snowy February afternoon, Neil took the bus to visit Sagan at Cornell University, in Ithaca, New York. They talked nonstop about science while Neil toured the labs, and then Sagan drove the high school senior through the snow back to the bus station. In case the bus had trouble with the snow and Neil needed a place to stay, Sagan gave Neil his home phone number.

Neil was touched. But he'd also heard many good things about Harvard University—and that's the school he chose.

In college, he stretched his muscles by wrestling, dancing, and running up and down every single path through the seats at the campus stadium. He stretched his brain by inhaling physics, mastering equations, and experimenting. And he stretched his wallet, earning money by writing, teaching, and tutoring.

After eleven more years of school, he earned the highest degree possible in astrophysics. He was literally one in a million. A star.

Neil kept looking up, continuing his research, solving mysteries. Then, at age thirty-five, he went to work at his beloved Hayden Planetarium, the very place where his dream had started. Eventually, he rose to become its director.

One day, a TV station asked him to appear as an expert. He was happy to explain that day's news about a solar flare, a small explosion on the sun. Afterward, Neil was jolted: "I'd never before in my life seen an interview with a black person on television for expertise that had nothing to do with being black."

He made it his mission to be visible, letting his enthusiasm explode in public. He wanted to infect others with his sense of awe and wonder at the universe—who *wouldn't* want to study it?

As he learned more and more new things in his research, it made him giddy, wanting to grab people on the street and say, "Have you heard this?"

Then it was time for the Hayden Planetarium to update its display of the planets. Neil met with other scientists and looked at the latest discoveries, and in 2000, they made a stunning decision. Pluto, then the smallest planet, would no longer be labeled as a planet in the new solar system display. They decided it had more in common with smaller, icy objects than it did with the other planets.

Neil got hate mail from Pluto lovers everywhere—but he showed that the frontier of science can change as new facts get discovered. Six years later, the International Astronomical Union agreed with him. Pluto was demoted to a dwarf planet.

No one has quite as much fun talking about science as Neil deGrasse Tyson. He is able to summon all that social energy his earliest teachers complained about. Fascinating facts tumble out, one explosion after another. He waves his hands and snaps his fingers. Laughter bubbles up, sometimes turning into a roar.

Equations are "awesome." The universe is "hilarious." Certain equations make him "misty." The sight of Saturn is simply "jaw-dropping." He uses a lot of exclamations, like "Whoa!"

He has a strong opinion on just about anything scientific, from the mystery of dark matter to the silliness of zombies.

"I have odd cosmic thoughts every day," he says.

Wearing one of his many star-themed ties (he has more than a hundred!), he never gets tired of appearing in public and dancing with words to describe science.

He also pours energy into articles, books, tweets, and TV appearances.

While Neil is rocking the world of science, he hangs on to his memory of being a small boy having his mind blown under a starry dome.

Sometimes, when he's in a remote area and sees all those stars, he thinks, *This looks just like the Hayden Planetarium!*

And when he goes outside, he still looks up: "I don't want to ever lose that. In life and in the universe, it's always best to keep looking up."

# Authors' Note

Neil deGrasse Tyson was born in 1958 in Manhattan. His mother, who is of Puerto Rican descent, nurtured her three children and later worked with the elderly for the US Department of Health. His African American father, a sociologist working for the City of New York, was active in the civil rights movement. Neil's middle name, "deGrasse," comes from a French admiral who fought for America in the Revolutionary War and had been imprisoned in the Caribbean. Neil's grandmother, who grew up on a Caribbean island, lived with the Tysons and constantly emphasized the importance of education.

Neil spent his first seventeen years living in the Bronx. After graduating from his prestigious high school, he earned a BA in physics from Harvard University, an MA in astronomy from the University of Texas at Austin, and a PhD in astrophysics from Columbia University. Since then, he has received honorary doctorates from twenty-two other universities. In 1994, Tyson joined the Hayden Planetarium as a staff scientist, and became its director in 1996, continuing his research and becoming famous as a marvelous speaker.

Among many other accomplishments, he served on two presidential commissions. He starred in the revival of *Cosmos*, the TV show made popular by his idol, Carl Sagan. He also has his own TV talk show, *StarTalk*, the first science-based talk show in television history.

Today he lives with his wife and family in Manhattan, tweets to his millions of followers, wears ties and vests with starry themes (to him it's like wearing the universe), and still uses a Saturn lamp he built in seventh grade.

# Sources

Browne, Rembert. "A Conversation with Neil deGrasse Tyson about 'Cosmos,' Race, and Celebrity." *Grantland*. June 9, 2014. grantland.com/hollywood-prospectus /a-conversation-with-neil-degrasse-tyson-about-cosmos-race-and-celebrity.

Hayden Planetarium at the American Museum of Natural History. amnh.org/our-research/hayden-planetarium.

Mead, Rebecca. "Starman." *The New Yorker*. February 17 and 24, 2014. newyorker.com/magazine/2014/02/17/starman.

"Neil deGrasse Tyson." Hayden Planetarium. haydenplanetarium.org/tyson/profile /about-neil-degrasse-tyson.

"Neil deGrasse Tyson." The Planetary Society.

Neil deGrasse Tyson's Twitter page. twitter.com/neiltyson.

"Pluto and the Developing Landscape of Our Solar System." International Astronomical Union. iau.org/public/themes/pluto.

Tyson, Neil deGrasse. *"A Brief History of Everything,* feat. Neil deGrasse Tyson." *ScienceAlert* video. July 21, 2015. sciencealert.com/watch-a-brief-history-of-everything-feat-neil-degrasse-tyson.

—. *Death by Black Hole and Other Cosmic Quandaries.* New York: Norton, 2007.

—. *The Pluto Files: The Rise and Fall of America's Favorite Planet.* New York: Norton, 2009.

—. *The Sky Is Not the Limit: Adventures of an Urban Astrophysicist.* Amherst, NY: Prometheus, 2004.

Tyson, Neil deGrasse, Charles Liu, and Robert Irion. *One Universe: At Home in the Cosmos.* Washington, DC: Joseph Henry Press, 2000.

Ventura, Marne. *Astrophysicist and Space Advocate: Neil DeGrasse Tyson.* STEM Trailblazer Bios. Minneapolis: Lerner, 2014.

YouTube, Neil deGrasse Tyson Interviews, youtube.com/channel /UC5DpYep7VSXseAEFr7UaEag, especially at Montclair Kimberly Academy with Stephen Colbert, youtube.com/watch?v=7BHQIasisqY.

To Emily Easton
—K.K. and P.B.

To my artist, technician, scientist son Nasir. Keep up your great works!
—F.M.

Text copyright © 2018 by Kathleen Krull and Paul Brewer
Jacket art and interior illustrations copyright © 2018 by Frank Morrison

All rights reserved. Published in the United States by Crown Books for Young Readers,
an imprint of Random House Children's Books, a division of Penguin Random House LLC, New York.

Crown and the colophon are registered trademarks of Penguin Random House LLC.

Visit us on the Web! rhcbooks.com

Educators and librarians, for a variety of teaching tools, visit us at
RHTeachersLibrarians.com

*Library of Congress Cataloging-in-Publication Data*
Names: Krull, Kathleen, author. | Brewer, Paul, author. | Morrison, Frank, illustrator.
Title: Starstruck: the cosmic journey of Neil deGrasse Tyson / by Kathleen Krull and Paul Brewer;
illustrated by Frank Morrison. | Description: First edition. | New York: Crown Books for Young Readers, [2018] |
Audience: Ages 4–8. | Audience: K to grade 3. | Identifiers: LCCN 2018011015 | ISBN 978-0-399-55024-9 (hc) |
ISBN 978-0-399-55025-6 (glb) | ISBN 978-0-399-55026-3 (epub) | Subjects: LCSH: Tyson, Neil deGrasse—
Juvenile literature. | Astrophysicists—United States—Biography—Juvenile literature. |
Classification: LCC QB460.72.T97 K78 2018 | DDC 523.01092 [B]—dc23

Book design by Nicole de las Heras

MANUFACTURED IN CHINA
10 9 8 7 6 5 4 3 2 1
First Edition

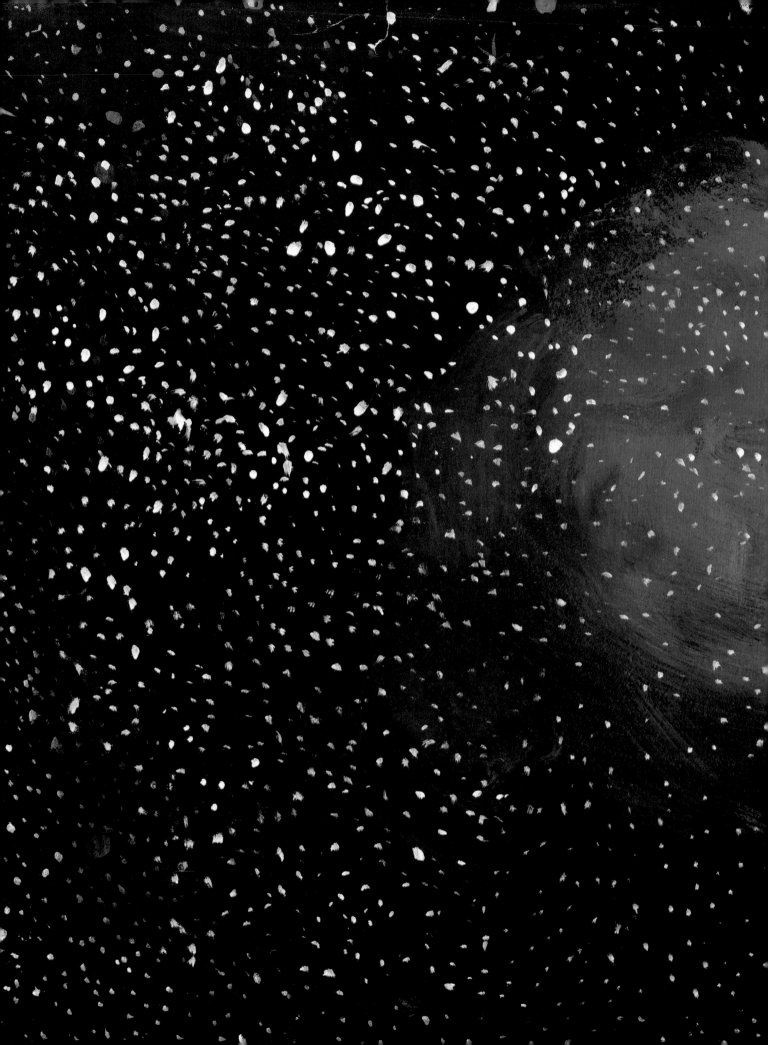